The Greatest Creation

A Book about the Beginning

Written by

Jessie Cleveland

Illustrated by

Donna Duchek

BluSky
PUBLISHERS.COM

Blue Sky Publishing

Copyright 2017 by Jessie Cleveland

Illustrations copyright 2017 by Donna Duchek

All rights reserved.

Published in the United States, 2018. Printed in Mexico.

ISBN: 978-0-692-99385-9

To get it just right, we'll start before light.

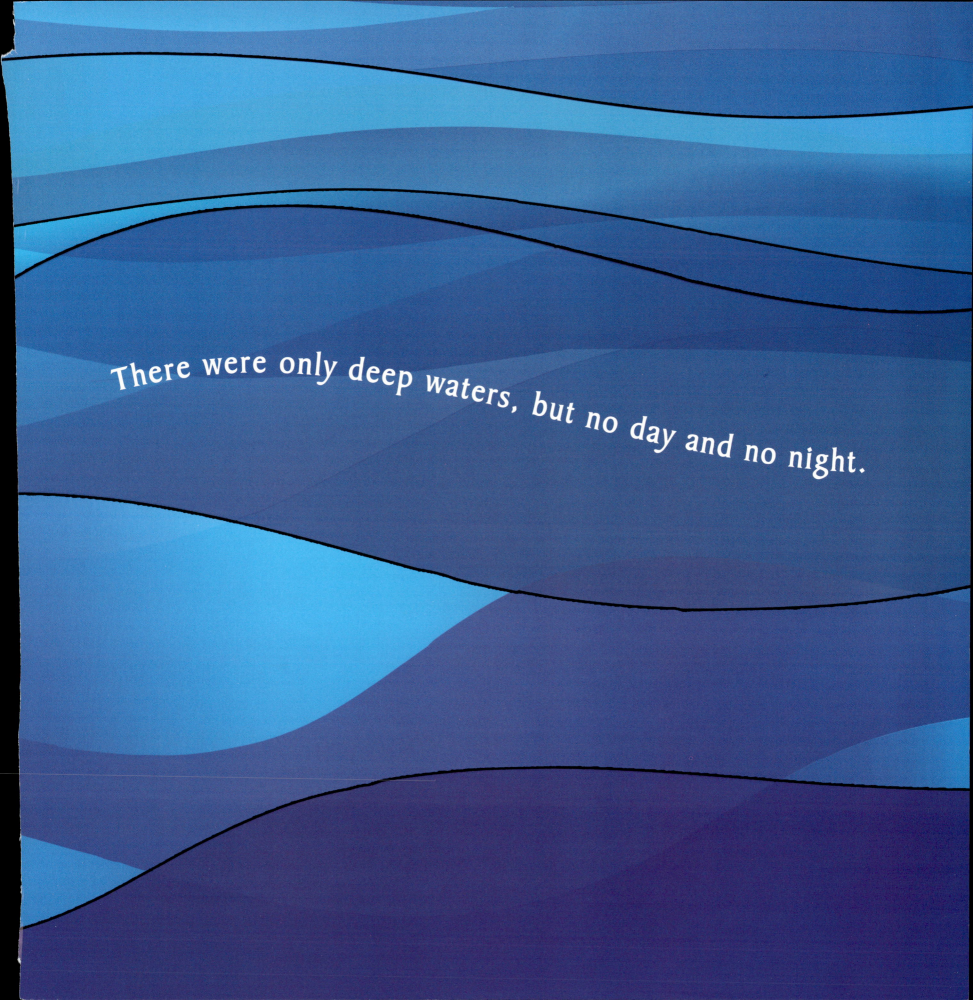
There were only deep waters, but no day and no night.

Above the waters lived God the creator.
He decided it was time to make something greater!

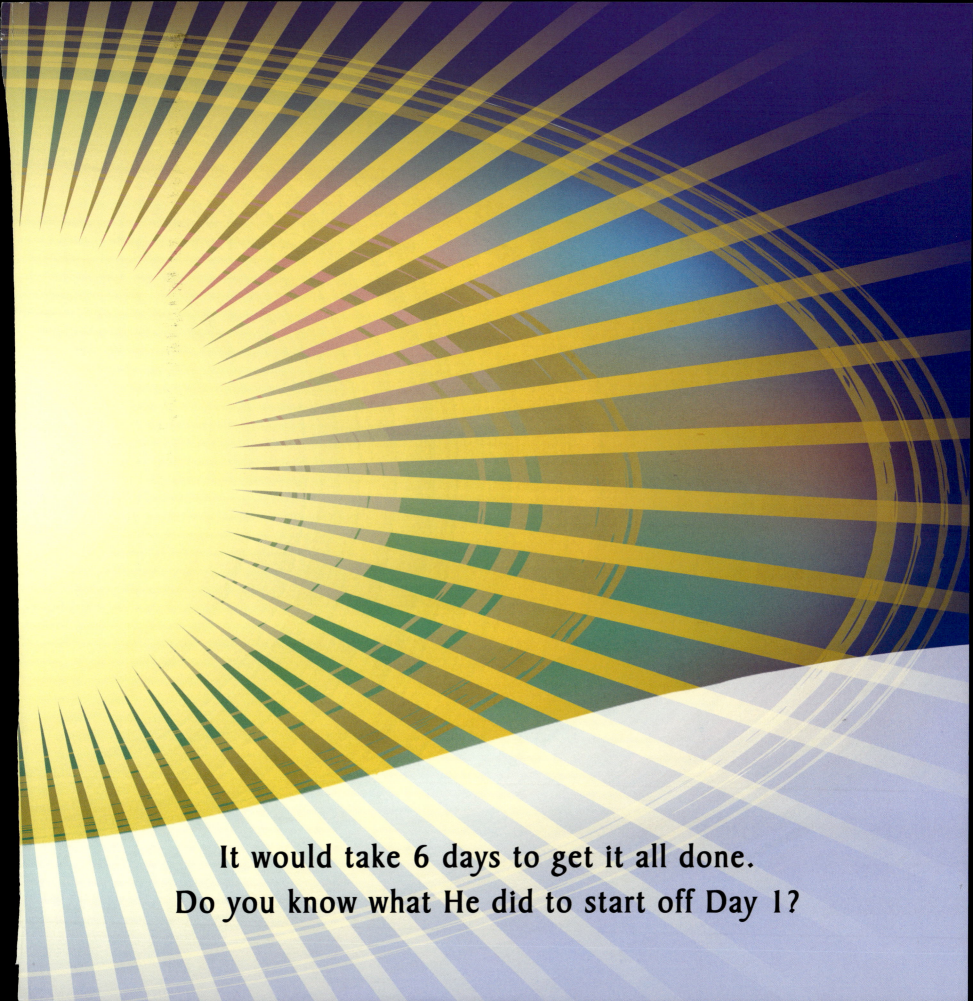

It would take 6 days to get it all done.
Do you know what He did to start off Day 1?

Out into the dark he said,
"Let there be light!"

He named the light Day,
and the dark He called Night.

...1

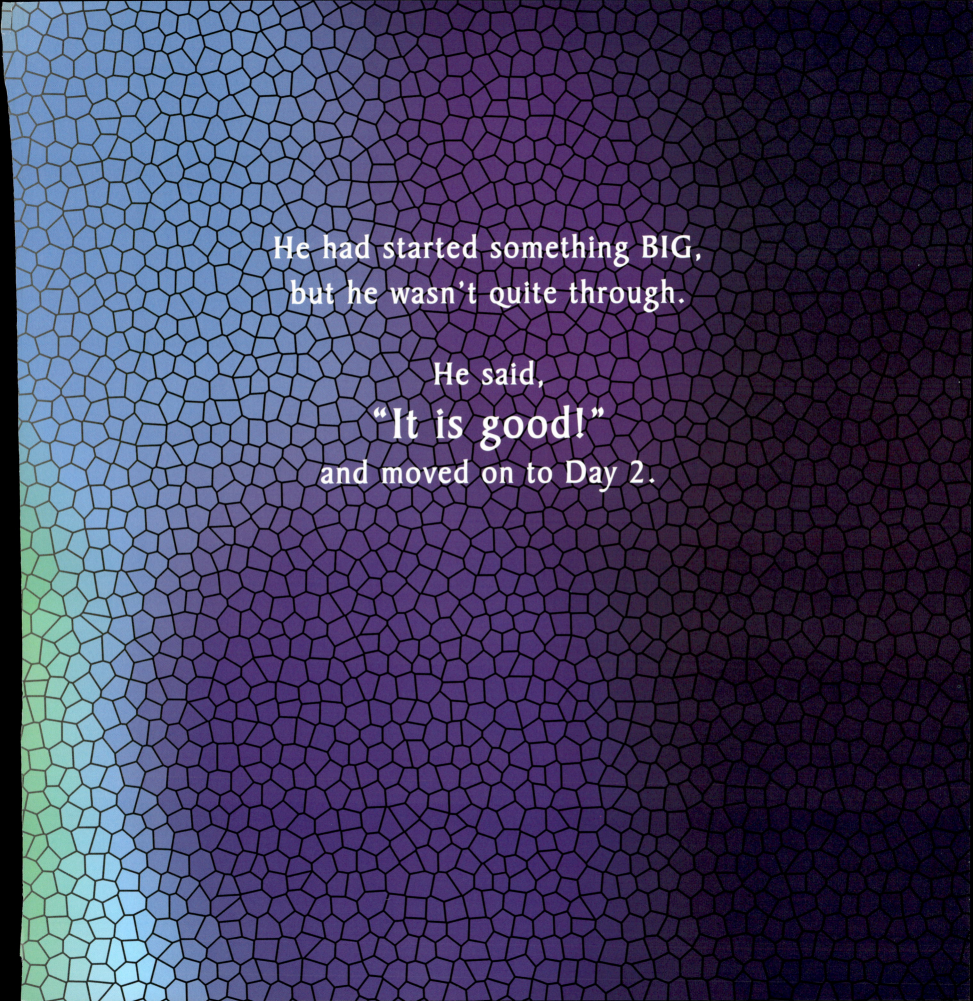

He had started something BIG,
but he wasn't quite through.

He said,
"It is good!"
and moved on to Day 2.

At the start of Day 2 it was all just too wet,
So He spoke out instructions to his best idea yet.

"There should be sky between heaven and sea!"
He stretched it all out and painted it blue as can be.

The sky is a big thing as you can see.
He said, "It is good!" and moved on to Day 3.

Where they come apart, we'll call them dry ground."

To the ground He commanded, "Grow up plants that will thrive."

He gave them all seeds to regrow and survive.

He admired his work from shore to shore. He said, "It is good!" and moved on to Day 4.

On Day 4 God decided to light our way, So he captured some of the light from the Day.

He formed the stars and moon for the night, And the Sun for the Day, He gave the most light.

4...

God also created the lights for more reasons. He said, "They will mark the days and years and even the seasons.

On Day 5 God created fish of the sea and birds of the sky.

From the deepest of deep to the highest of high.

He filled up the oceans, streams, rivers, and lakes.
From the top to the bottom He made no mistakes.

5...

With the waters all filled he looked to the sky.
He called for the song birds, the eagles,
and all things that fly.

With creatures flying and swimming and doing cool tricks,
He said, "It is good!" and moved on to Day 6.

On Day 6 God had a busy day planned.
With animals and people he would fill up dry land!

First He made animals both big and small.
From elephants to snails, God created them all.

God had spoken out every living creature.
Each with its own unique feature.

But God had one more thing to create.
Next He used His hands to make something great.

"Let's make people in Our image."
He began to plan.
From the dirt in the ground He formed up a man.

Into the man's nose He breathed in life.
Then He decided the man needed a wife.

While the man slept, God borrowed a bone.
From the chest bone of a man a woman was grown.

6...

To the man and the woman God gave
all He'd created.
"I made all these things for you," He stated.

God watched over it all from Heaven.
He said, "It is VERY good!"
and moved on to Day 7.

On Day 7
God chose to take a good rest.
He had worked hard for 6 days doing His best.

He created plants, animals, and human beings.
He used His imagination to create millions of things.

So go for a walk under a sky that is blue.
And look all around at what God created for you!

Dedicated to people everywhere who want to know God better.